125 Brain Games
for Babies

Other books by Jackie Silberg

Games to Play With Babies
Games to Play With Toddlers
Games to Play With Two Year Olds
More Games to Play With Toddlers
300 Three Minute Games
500 Five Minute Games
The I Can't Sing Book

Jackie Silberg is an acclaimed speaker, teacher, and trainer on both early childhood development and music. You can arrange to have her speak, present, train, or entertain by contacting her through Gryphon House, PO Box 207, Beltsville MD 20704-0207
or
at jsilberg@interserv.com.

125 Brain Games for Babies

simple games to promote early brain development

Jackie Silberg

gryphon
house
Beltsville, Maryland

Dedication

This book is dedicated to all of the lucky people who spend time with babies. The joy, the challenge, and the great satisfaction that you can help "grow" a baby's brain will make your life more meaningful each day. And by the way, give your baby a big kiss from me.

Acknowledgments

To my editor, Kathy Charner–this is our eighth book together, and the wonderful friendship that we have developed is very meaningful to me. To Leah and Larry Rood, the owners and publishers of Gryphon House, thank you for your constant support and great kindness. To all of the staff at Gryphon House for your consistent help and inventive ideas that make my books so successful.

Copyright © 1999 Jackie Silberg
Published by Gryphon House, Inc.
10726 Tucker Street, Beltsville MD 20705
Visit us on the web at www.gryphonhouse. com

Text illustration by: Becky Malone

Library of Congress Cataloging-in-Publication Data

Silberg, Jackie, 1934-
    125 brain games for babies simple games to promote early brain
    development / Jackie Silberg.
        p.   cm.
    Includes bibliographical references and index.
    ISBN 0-87659-199-3
    1. Ability in infants. 2. Ability in children. 3. Intellect-
Problems, exercises, etc. 4. Learning, Psychology of—Problems,
exercises, etc. 5. Infant psychology. 6. Child psychology.
I. Title. II. Title: One hundred twenty-five brain games for babies.
BF720.A24S57 1999
649'.122—dc2l   99-17317
                                                               CIP

Table of Contents

Introduction

My two-month-old grandson is a joy to play with. His coos and smiles melt my heart. He dearly loves to be held and rocked and nuzzled and cuddled. In the past my reaction to all this was "Isn't he sweet?" or "Isn't he precious?" Now I think about him differently. He is still very sweet and precious, but now I know that cuddling and rocking and singing and nuzzling will help his brain grow.

By the time a child is three, the brain has formed 1000 trillion connections—about twice as many as adults have. Some brain cells, called neurons, have already been hard-wired to other cells before birth. They control the baby's heartbeat, breathing, and reflexes and regulate other functions essential to survival. The rest of the brain connections are waiting to be "hooked up."

The connections neurons make with each other are called synapses. While various parts of the brain develop at different rates, study after study has shown that the peak production period for synapses is from birth to about age 10. During that time, the receptive branches of the nerve cells, called dendrites, are growing and reaching out to form trillions upon trillions of synapses. One cell can be connected to 10,000 other cells. The brain's weight triples to nearly adult size. Periods of rapid synapse production in specific parts of the brain seem to correspond to the development of behaviors linked to those parts of the brain. Scientists believe the stimulation that babies and young children receive determines which synapses form in the brain—that is, which pathways become hard-wired.

How does the brain know which connections to keep? This is where early experience comes into play. When a connection is used repeatedly in the early years, it becomes permanent. Conversely, a connection that is not used at all or often enough, is unlikely to survive. For example, a child who is rarely spoken to or read to in the early years may have difficulty mastering language skills later on. A child who is rarely played with may have difficulty with social adjustment as she grows. An infant's brain thrives on feedback from its environment. It wires itself into a thinking and emotional organ from the things it experiences. The circuits that form in the brain influence the development of a child. Chances are a child submerged in language from birth will learn to speak very well. A baby whose coos are met with smiles, rather than apathy, will likely become emotionally responsive.

Scientists have learned more in the past ten years about how the human brain works than in all of previous history. Their discovery that early childhood experiences profoundly shape the infant brain is changing the way we think about the needs of children.

Recent brain research has produced three key findings. First, an individual's capacity to learn and thrive in a variety of settings depends on the interplay between nature (their genetic endowment) and nurture (the kind of care, stimulation, and teaching they receive). Second, the human brain is uniquely constructed to benefit from experience and from good teaching during the first years of life. And third, while the opportunities and risks are greatest during the first years of life, learning takes place throughout the human life cycle.

The very best way to develop a baby's brain connections is to do what babies need, starting with caring, attentive parents and caregivers. Babies need an environment that is interesting to explore, that is safe, and that is filled with people who will respond to their emotional and intellectual needs. People who will sing to them, hug them, talk to them, rock them, read to them—not flash cards in front of their faces. All these brain connections are not meant to push early learning but rather to develop the potential for future learning. When brain development happens as it should, future learning is likely to be successful. All the games in this book develop the brain capacity of babies. They are the building blocks of future learning—a good, solid beginning for babies. And they are fun, too!

Writing this book has been an exciting experience for me. I think that everyone who has been around babies senses the amazing capacities that they have. Now science has supported so many of the things that we already know intuitively. Every time I play with a baby and I see her shake a set of keys, pound on a table, or reach out to grasp something from my hand, I think, "Wow, she's making connections in her brain." I hope this book will help you create a lot of "Wow" times with your baby.

Birth to 3 Months

1

The more gentle the stimulation you give an infant, the greater the number of brain synapses and connections that are formed.

Newborn Games

- Infants as young as one day old recognize the voices of their parents. If you patted your tummy and talked to your baby while she was in the womb, she will know the sound of your voice.

- While your infant is lying on her back, walk to one side of the crib and call out her name.

- Keep saying her name until she moves her eyes or her head toward the sound.

- Walk to the other side of the crib and say her name again.

- Gently massage her body as you smile into her eyes and say her name.

Snuggle Buggle, I Love You

2

Research shows that the more an infant is cuddled, snuggled, and held, the more secure and independent she will be when she is older.

- Hold your baby in your arms and rock her back and forth.
- As you rock, say the words, "Snuggle, buggle, I love you."
- On the word "you" kiss a part of her body—head, nose, toes.
- As your child grows older, she may ask to play this game.
- This game develops bonding.

**WHAT BRAIN
RESEARCH SAYS**

Babies respond
to "parentese" —
the high-pitched
sounds adults
make when talk-
ing to babies.

Baby Talk

- When you speak "parentese" to infants, you are communicating with them and encouraging vocal responses. This in turn develops language skills.

- Say things like, "You're such a sweet baby" or "Look at those ten little toes."

- As you speak in parentese, hold the baby near to your face and look directly into her eyes.

Soothing Music

**WHAT BRAIN
RESEARCH SAYS**

Newborns
possess a
natural response
to music
through their
conditioning in
the womb to
rhythm, sound,
and movement.

■ Place a small cassette player near your baby's crib.

■ Choose soft instrumental music or lullabies to play.

■ Music that has a repeated melody is very soothing to an infant because it is the kind of sound she heard in the womb.

■ Tape the sounds of your dishwasher and play it for your baby. This sound is also similar to the sounds of the womb.

The Blowing Game

**WHAT BRAIN
RESEARCH SAYS**

Research shows
that positive
sensory experi-
ences and social
interactions with
adults advance
babies' cogni-
tive abilities.

- This game helps an infant become aware of the different parts of her body.

- Blow gently on your baby's palms. As you blow, say the following words in a singsong chant:

   Here are the baby's palms.

- Then kiss your baby's palms.

- Blow on other parts of the body. Most babies like gentle blowing on their elbows, fingers, neck, cheek, and toes.

Nonverbal Games

WHAT BRAIN RESEARCH SAYS

Touching, holding, and cuddling a baby not only comforts her, but helps her brain grow.

■ Communicate with infants by looking into their eyes, holding them close to your body, and responding to their sounds.

■ Holding your baby close to you develops the secure attachment that she needs for her growth.

■ Hold your baby close and walk around the room.

■ Stop walking and look into her eyes, smile, and rub noses.

■ Start walking again, then stop. Repeat this several times.

BIRTH TO 3 MONTHS

7

WHAT BRAIN RESEARCH SAYS

A child's capacity to control emotions hinges on early experiences and attach-ments.

Hugs and Kisses

■ How we touch, treat, and nurture infants can have a deep effect on the kind of adults they become. This game will make your baby feel safe and secure.

■ Chant the following song as you rock and kiss your baby:

Hugs and kisses, I love you
I love you, I love you
Hugs and kisses, I love you
You're my baby.

■ When you are diapering your baby, you can sing this song and kiss her nose, her toes, her fingers.

Here's My Finger

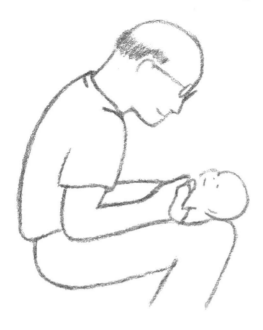

WHAT BRAIN RESEARCH SAYS

Just reaching for an object helps the brain develop hand-eye coordination.

- This game strengthens a baby's hands and fingers.

- Hold your infant in your lap.

- Put your index finger in your baby's hand.

- She probably will grasp your finger, as this is a natural reflex with newborns.

- Each time she grasps your finger, say positive words like, "That's my wonderful girl!" or "You're so strong!"

- This game also develops tracking skills.

9

At birth your baby can see best between eight and twelve inches from her eyes.

Hello

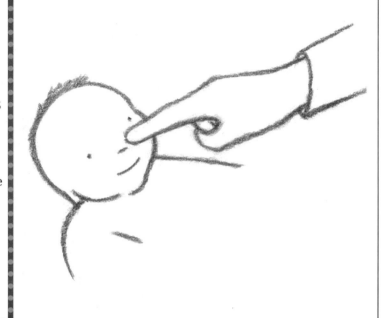

■ When your baby sees your face, she will be content.

■ Say the following poem with your face close to your baby's face:

> *Hello, hello, I love you very much.*
>
> *Hello, hello, my fingers they can touch.*
>
> *Hello, hello, I'll touch your little nose.*
> *(touch baby's nose)*
>
> *Hello, hello, I'll kiss your little nose.*
> *(kiss baby's nose)*

■ Repeat this poem and change the last two lines to different parts of baby's face—ears, eyes, cheek, lips.

Where Did It Go?

WHAT BRAIN RESEARCH SAYS

Neurons for vision begin forming during the first few months of life. Activities that stimulate a baby's sight will insure good visual development.

- Hold a brightly colored scarf in front of your baby.

- Slowly move it around and talk about how bright it is.

- When you are sure that your baby is looking at the scarf, slowly move it to one side.

- Keep moving it back and forth to encourage her to follow it with her eyes.

- Play this game often. You are helping your baby's brain capacity grow!

Note: As with any game, watch for signs that your baby may be tired of the game and ready to rest or play something different.

11

WHAT BRAIN
RESEARCH SAYS

By two months
babies can
distinguish
features on a
face.

Follow the Action

■ Babies love to look at faces, especially faces of people they love.

■ Try different facial expressions and sounds to develop your baby's vision and hearing.

■ Here are some ideas:

✓ Sing a song and use big movements with your mouth.

✓ Blink your eyes.

✓ Stick out your tongue.

✓ Make contortions with your mouth.

✓ Make lip sounds.

✓ Cough or yawn.

The Rattle Game

■ Hold a rattle in front of your baby and shake it gently.

■ As you shake the rattle, sing any song or the following to the tune of "Old MacDonald":

Rattle, rattle, shake, shake, shake, E-I-E-I-O

Rattle, rattle, shake, shake, shake, E-I-E-I-O

■ When you are sure that your baby is watching the rattle, slowly move it to one side and sing the song again.

■ Continue moving the rattle to different places in the room and watch as your baby moves her head in the direction of the sound.

■ Put the rattle in your baby's hand and sing the song again.

■ Babies love singing and later, when they are ready to talk, they will try to imitate sounds they've heard.

13

A one-month-old baby can see as far away as three feet and is very interested in the environment.

The Hat Game

- Your face is one of the first things your baby recognizes.

- Try playing the hat game with your infant. She will recognize your face and you will be stimulating her vision.

- Select different hats to put on your head. As you put on the different hats, say the following:

> *Hats, hats, hats, hats (slowly shake your head back and forth)*
>
> *(Mommy, Daddy, name of person) has a hat*
>
> *(same person) loves (name of baby)*
>
> *When she (he) wears her (his) hat.*

- If you don't have many hats, put a scarf or ribbon on your head.

Sensory Experiences

What babies see and smell cause brain connections to be made, especially if the experiences happen in a loving, consistent, predictable manner.

■ Exposing your baby to many different sensations will broaden her awareness of herself and the world.

■ Try rubbing your baby's arms with different fabrics. Satin, wool, and terrycloth are good fabrics to start with.

■ Give your baby an opportunity to experience different smells. Go outside and smell a flower. Smell a freshly cut orange.

Note: Be careful not to overstimulate your baby. Watch for signs that your baby is tired of the game.

15

The neurons for vision begin to form around two months. Stimulating vision will help make the visual connections.

Shadows

- Infants wake up many times during the night.

- Shadows cast on the wall by a nightlight make interesting shapes and forms for your baby to look at.

- If you can arrange a mobile so that it reflect shadows, you will be helping to develop your baby's visual growth.

- When your child gets a little older, make shadow designs with your hands.

Be a Baby

WHAT BRAIN RESEARCH SAYS

Positive emotional, physical, and intellectual experiences are critical for the growth of a healthy brain.

- If you want to have a better insight into your baby's perspective, try being a baby yourself.

- Investigate the world as your baby does.

- Lie on your back and look at the world as your baby does.

- What do you see, hear, and smell?

- Move to a different place and look, listen, and smell.

- Doing this kind of activity will give you many ideas of games to play with your baby that will encourage her development.

The Turning Game

**WHAT BRAIN
RESEARCH SAYS**

Exposing babies
to different
visual fields will
develop hand-
eye coordina-
tion and
balance, both
of which are
prerequisites for
crawling and
walking.

■ Turning your infant in different directions will help her
  develop an awareness of space and a sense of balance.

■ Try turning your infant in the following ways:

  ✓ Hold her in your arms and support her head as
    you turn in circles.

  ✓ Hold her with her back against your body.

  ✓ Carry her with her face looking at yours.

■ As you turn with her in different directions, sing nursery
  rhymes.

Bicycle

**WHAT BRAIN
RESEARCH SAYS**

An infant's brain
thrives on feed-
back from its
environment
and "wires"
itself into a
thinking and
emotional organ
based on early
experiences.

■ Put your baby on her back and move her legs like she is
riding a bicycle.

Note: Never force your baby's legs. If she resists, try something else.

■ Sing bicycle songs like "A Bicycle Built for Two" as you
move her legs.

■ Try making up a simple song. Here's an idea that can be
sung to the tune of "Row, Row, Row Your Boat":

> *Ride, ride, ride your bike*
> *Up and down the street.*
> *Happily, happily, happily, happily*
> *This is such a treat.*

Bend Those Knees

WHAT BRAIN
RESEARCH SAYS

Strengthening
your baby's
thigh muscles is
important for
future crawling
and walking.

- Place your baby on her back and carefully pull both legs until they are straight.

- When her legs are straight, lightly tap the bottoms of her feet.

- She will point her toes downward and bend her knees.

- As you do this game, sing the following to the tune of "Ring Around the Rosy":

  Bending, bending, bending
  Little knees are bending
  Bending, bending
  Hip hooray!

- End a rhyme with some kind of a cheer. Your baby will learn to anticipate it, and it makes the game more exciting.

Tongue Tales

WHAT BRAIN RESEARCH SAYS

Talking to a baby starts "wiring" the neurons from her ears to connect with the auditory part of the brain.

- Hold your baby in your arms.

- Look into her eyes and stick out your tongue. While it is sticking out, make silly noises.

- Put your tongue back in.

- Repeat the above and make a different sound.

- Very young babies will often try to stick out their tongues.

21

**WHAT BRAIN
RESEARCH SAYS**

Communicating
with your baby
helps brain
neurons make
the connections
for language
development.

Staring

- Staring at your baby is a fun thing to do. Your little one will stare right back at you.

- When you are sure that you have her attention, change the expression on your face. Smile, make a sound, or wiggle your nose.

- Enjoy your baby's reaction as she watches your face. She will probably get excited by widening her eyes or starting to move her arms or legs.

Switching Pitches

When babies are in the womb, they are able to distinguish the sound of human voices.

■ According to brain research, when a baby hears a high-pitched voice (like "parentese"), her heart rate increases, indicating that she feels secure and cheerful.

■ When you speak in a lower pitched voice, your baby feels soothed and content.

■ Try singing a song in a high voice and then repeat the same song in a low voice. Watch the reaction of your baby to the two different sounds.

**WHAT BRAIN
RESEARCH SAYS**

Singing to
babies facilitates
genuine bond-
ing between
adult and child.

Diaper Songs

■ Singing to your baby while you change a diaper is a lovely
way to communicate and bond with your little one.

■ Smile while you are singing.

■ Sing any song you know or sing the following to the tune
of "London Bridge":

> *Change a diaper, just like this*
> *Just like this,*
> *Just like this.*
> *Change a diaper, just like this*
> *Clean, clean, baby.*

Talking to Baby

WHAT BRAIN RESEARCH SAYS

The more you talk to your baby, the more her brain will make important connections for language.

- Talk about everything that you are doing. Describe what you are doing when you are washing your hands, getting dressed, etc.

- Recite poetry and nursery rhymes, and sing songs throughout the day.

- From time to time, vary the sound of your voice. Try talking in a high voice, low voice, singsong voice, and soft voice.

A Diaper Game

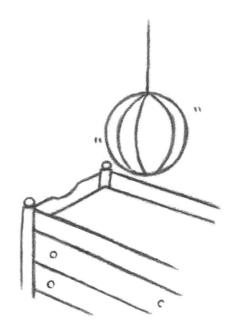

- The changing table is always a good place for developing motor skills.

- Why not give your baby interesting things to look at while she is being changed?

- Try hanging an inflatable ball from the ceiling close enough for you to reach, but out of baby's reach.

- Make the ball move slowly while you are changing the diaper.

- Your baby will be fascinated by this and, before long, will try to reach out and touch the ball.

- When the diaper is changed, hold your baby and let her touch the ball.

- You could also hang a mobile with family pictures from the ceiling.

Roll Over

26

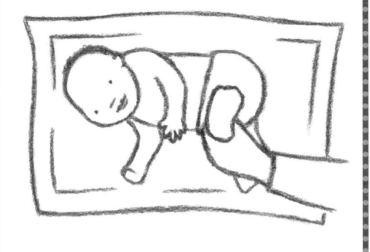

■ Lay your baby on her back on a soft surface.

■ Hold her ankle and thigh on the same side and cross this leg over the other leg. Don't worry, her hips and torso will follow.

Note: Never force this movement.

■ Return her to her original position.

■ Do the same with the other leg, crossing over in the other direction.

■ As you do the crossing over, say

> *There were two in the bed*
>
> *And the little one said,*
>
> *Roll over, roll over.*
> *(cross the legs when you say this part)*
>
> *And they all crossed over.*

27

Roll, Roll

- Large inflatable balls are wonderful props to use with infants.

- One way to use this kind of ball is to place your baby on the ball.

- With her tummy on the ball and your hands holding her securely, slowly roll the ball back and forth.

- While you are rolling, sing a song such as the following to the tune of "Row, Row, Row Your Boat":

  Roll, roll, roll the ball

  Back and forth we go.

  Merrily, merrily, merrily, merrily

  Back and forth we go.

- This rocking motion is very relaxing for an infant.

3 to 6 Months

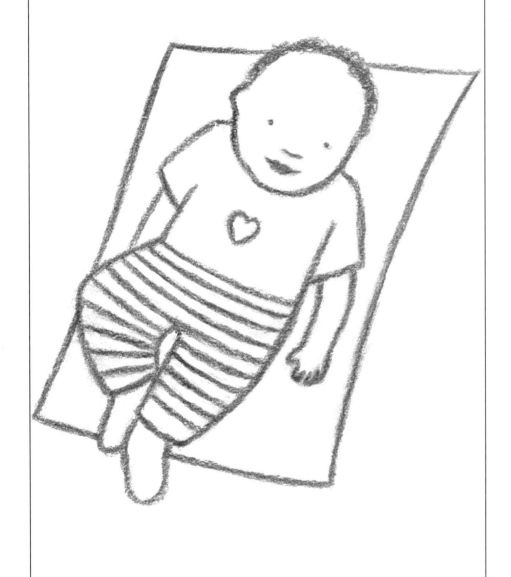

28

WHAT BRAIN
RESEARCH SAYS

Exercising visual
skills is essential
during the first
six months of
life.

Look What I See

- Babies love to stare at interesting faces and toys.

- Take several colorful toys and, one at a time, slowly move them back and forth in front of your baby to stimulate his vision.

- This is also the time when babies discover their hands. They watch and watch and finally discover that they can make them appear and disappear.

- Take your baby's hands and gently clap them in front of his face. As you do this, say the following poem:

    Clap, clap, clap your hands,

    Clap your hands together.

    Put your hands on Mommy's face. (substitute name of the person doing the rhyme with baby)

    Clap your hands together.

Who Is That Baby?

Short utterances speed up the development of the language process.

- Sit in front of a mirror with your baby in your lap.

- Say, "Who is that baby?"

- Wave your baby's hand and say, "Hi, baby."

- Say, "Where's the baby's foot?"

- Wave your baby's foot and say, "Hi, foot."

- Continue asking questions and moving different parts of your baby's body.

- Shake heads, wave bye-bye, clap hands, etc.

**WHAT BRAIN
RESEARCH SAYS**

Babies need a
large variety of
tactile experi-
ences to
become familiar
with their world.

Tap, Tap, Tap

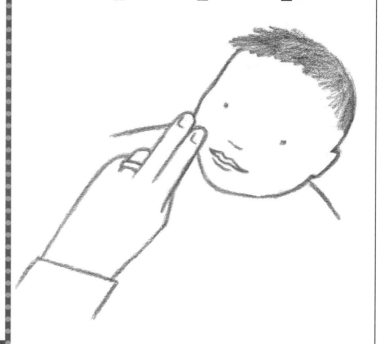

■ Try playing this tapping game with your baby.

■ Using your index and middle finger, gently tap on different parts of his body. As you tap, name the part of the body.

■ Use the following poem as a guide:

Tap, tap, tap

On my baby's (or use baby's name) cheek.

Tap, tap, tap

*On my baby's cheek. (take his
hand and put it on his cheek)*

■ Repeat this little poem, tapping different parts of the body.

■ Reverse the game. Take your baby's fingers and tap them on your body.

Let's Watch

**WHAT BRAIN
RESEARCH SAYS**

Loving care
provides a
baby's brain
with positive
emotional
stimulation.

■ Think of all the different places that are good for watching.

■ If babies can watch things move, they are happy.

■ A front-loading washing machine or dryer is fun for babies
to watch.

■ Windows that are close to trees are wonderful watching
places, or sit outside with your baby for an amazing
amount of stimulation.

✓ Watch birds fly from one place to another.

✓ Watch cars moving down the street.

✓ Watch the branches of a tree blow in the wind.

■ Take time to sit with your child and watch together. Having
you next to him will give him the comfort and security that
he needs to enjoy the wonders of the world.

Nuggle Nose

**WHAT BRAIN
RESEARCH SAYS**

Gently touching
your baby will
make him feel
secure and safe,
enabling him
to become
confident and,
eventually,
independent.

- Hold your baby in the air and say, "Nose, nose, nuggle nose."

- On the word "nuggle," bring him down and touch your nose to his.

- Keep repeating this game touching noses on the word "nuggle."

- After you have played this a few times, say the word "nuggle" more than one time, always touching noses on the word "nuggle."

- For example, say "nuggle, nuggle, nuggle, nose."

Where's My Baby ?

WHAT BRAIN RESEARCH SAYS

Developing strength and balance lays the groundwork for crawling.

- This is a game that strengthens the back and neck.

- Lie on your back and put your baby on your tummy.

- With your hands firmly around his chest, raise him in the air and up to your face.

- Say the following and do the actions:

  Where's my baby?

  There he is. (lift him up to your face)

  Where's my baby? (bring him back down to your tummy)

  There he is. (bring him back up to your face)

  Where's my baby? (bring him back down to your tummy)

  Up high, high, high. (bring your baby up high over your face)

WHAT BRAIN RESEARCH SAYS

Exercising helps the brain refine the circuits for motor skill development.

Uppity Uppity Up

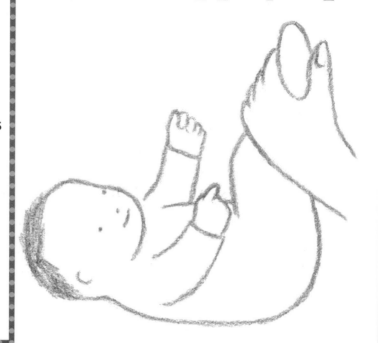

- Exercising your baby's arms and legs will help develop his muscles and motor coordination.

- This is a good game to play when your baby is on his back.

- Gently lift up one leg at a time and say this rhyme:

    Uppity up, uppity up

    One, two, down. (put his foot down)

Note: Never force any movement. If your baby resists, try this another time.

- Repeat with the other foot.

- Repeat with each arm.

- Do both feet at the same time.

- Then do both arms at the same time.

Leg Game

WHAT BRAIN RESEARCH SAYS

Exercise strengthens large muscles to prepare babies for walking.

■ Lay your baby on his back on a firm surface.

■ Holding his ankles, bend and straighten his legs to the following rhyme:

> *One, two, three,*
> *Bend your knees.*
> *One, two, three,*
> *Bend your knees.*

Note: If your baby resists, stop immediately. Never force any movement.

■ Sing the words above to a familiar tune, or make up your own tune. It will capture your baby's attention and develop his language at the same time.

Going Up the Escalator

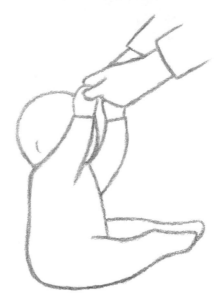

■ Hold onto baby's fingers and gently lift baby's arms as you say the following rhyme:

> *Going up the escalator*
> *Up, up, up.*
> *Going down the escalator*
> *Down, down, down.*

■ Lift your baby's legs and say the rhyme.

■ Continue lifting different parts of your baby's body, saying the rhyme each time.

■ Try ending with lifting him up in the air and down.

■ Always give a kiss on the down part.

Talking Together

WHAT BRAIN RESEARCH SAYS

A baby whose coos and gurgles are met with smiles will likely become emotionally responsive.

- At this age babies often make lots of sounds. Mimic the sounds that your baby makes. Those simple sounds will later turn into words.

- Take the words that your baby makes, such as "ba ba" or "ma ma," and turn them into sentences. "Ma ma loves you." "Ba ba says the sheep."

- Penelope Leach, a child development expert, says, "Your child may say hundreds of different sounds throughout the day but if you clap and applaud when he says, 'ma ma' or 'da da', he will keep repeating those sounds because it makes you happy."

- The more you repeat your baby's sounds, the more he will be encouraged to make more sounds.

- This is truly the beginning of a conversation.

Taping Sounds

**WHAT BRAIN
RESEARCH SAYS**

Babies just four days old can distinguish one language from another and soon pay attention to the sounds (words) that matter.

- Tape record your baby's babbling.

- Play the sounds of the tape and see how he responds.

- Do the sounds get your baby excited? Does he talk back to the tape recorder?

- If your baby enjoys listening to the taped sounds, try other ones like nature sounds.

- This kind of stimulating environment assures good language skills for the future.

Connect With Conversation

The number of words an infant hears each day influence his or her future intelligence, social graces, and scholastic achievements.

■ Start a conversation with your baby. Say a short sentence like, "It is a beautiful day today."

■ When your baby responds with some babble or a coo, stop talking and look into his eyes.

■ As he talks, respond with a nod of your head or a smile.

■ This indicates to your baby that you are listening to him and enjoying his sounds.

■ Continue with another sentence. Always stop and listen to your baby's response.

■ When you let your baby know that you are listening to him and that you like what he says, you are developing his language skills and confidence.

40

WHAT BRAIN
RESEARCH SAYS

Responsive
"conversation"
builds a baby's
vocabulary.

Read My Lips

■ At three months, your baby may be making lots of wonderful sounds. When you respond to his sounds, you encourage him to talk even more.

■ As you repeat the sounds that he is making, put his fingers to your lips and let him feel the movement as well as the air coming from your mouth.

■ Put your fingers to his lips and encourage him to make more sounds.

Ba Ba Baby-O

WHAT BRAIN RESEARCH SAYS

Talking and singing to a baby significantly speed up the process of learning new words.

- Sing any song using one sound instead of words.

- Pick a sound that your baby is making—probably ma or ba.

- Sing songs using just those sounds with a few words.

- For example, sing the following to the tune of "Old MacDonald":

  Ba ba ba ba ba baby
  Ba ba ba ba O
  Ba ba ba ba ba baby
  Ba ba ba ba O

- Other songs that you could sing are "Twinkle Twinkle Little Star," "The Muffin Man," and "Humpty Dumpty."

- The more that you repeat the sounds your baby is making, the more sounds your baby will make.

42

Repeating motor skills over and over strengthens the neural circuits that go from the brain's thinking areas to the motor areas and out to the nerves that move muscles.

Let's Kick

■ Kicking develops motor skills and is something that babies love to do.

■ Attach colorful items to your baby's ankles and watch him kick with glee.

■ Many booties have brightly colored toes that babies love to watch as they kick.

■ Hold your baby in your arms and dangle a rattle or bells in front of his feet.

■ Show him how to kick the rattle or bells.

Roll Olympics

WHAT BRAIN RESEARCH SAYS

Using these muscles repeatedly gives babies' muscles the strength and elasticity for rolling over.

■ Helping your baby roll over from his tummy to his back will develop his chest and arm muscles. This is a fun game to play while encouraging your baby to roll over.

■ Put your baby on his tummy on a soft and flat surface. Carpeted floors and the middle of beds are good for this game.

■ Hold up a teddy bear in front of his face and do antics with the bear. You might say the following poem as you make the teddy bear move around:

> *Teddy bear, teddy bear, turn a round.*
> *(turn teddy bear around)*
>
> *Teddy bear, teddy bear, touch the ground.*
> *(make teddy fall down)*

■ When you know that your baby is watching the teddy, move it to the side so that your baby's eyes and hopefully his body will follow it.

■ Repeat the poem, moving the teddy bear each time. If your baby tires of this game, try it again on another day.

WHAT BRAIN RESEARCH SAYS

Connecting rhythm, movement, and bonding produce lots of brain "wiring" that likely will help babies in their future development.

Dance a Baby

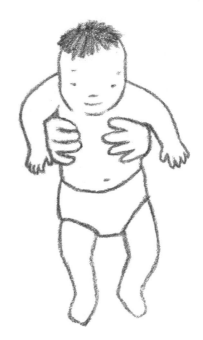

- This is a variation of an old English rhyme called "Dance a Baby Diddy."

- Hold your baby firmly under his arms and dance him on a soft surface.

- Say the rhyme and do the actions.

> *Dance a baby diddy*
> *What can I do widdy?*
> *Sit on a lap. (put baby on your lap)*
> *And give him a pat. (gently pat his cheek)*
> *Dance a baby diddy, dance a baby diddy.*
> *(go back to dancing)*

Pop Goes the Weasel

WHAT BRAIN RESEARCH SAYS

Exposure to music "wires" neural circuits in the brain.

- Babies enjoy music and rhythm. When they were in the womb, they felt the rhythm of the heart and sounds of the blood moving in the body.

- Take two rhythm sticks (or two wooden spoons) and tap them together as you sing the song "Pop Goes the Weasel."

- Tap the sticks softly and increase the loudness of the sound when you come to the word "pop." Soon your baby will begin to anticipate the louder sound.

- Help your baby hold the sticks. Sing the song while he is holding the sticks.

  All around the cobbler's bench

  The monkey chased the weasel.

  The monkey laughed to see such fun.

  Pop! goes the weasel.

Hup, Two, Three, Four

WHAT BRAIN RESEARCH SAYS

Singing and dancing with your baby is one of the best things that you can do to help "wire" his brain.

- Hold your baby close to your body and move around the room as you sing your favorite songs. Any song will do as long as it's a song that you like and enjoy.

- Your baby will sense your joy and this makes him happy, too.

- Try a marching cadence and say the words "hup, two, three, four" as you march around the room.

- You can also sway, turn, tiptoe, and take large, sweeping steps.

Let's Bounce

47

WHAT BRAIN RESEARCH SAYS

Bouncing and rocking is a prerequisite for crawling.

■ Bouncing games are such fun for babies and they play an important role in helping little ones learn to balance, which is a prerequisite for walking.

■ You can bounce your baby in many ways—sitting on your lap, laying with his tummy on your knees, laying on his back on your knees, sitting on your lap and rocking side to side.

Note: Always support your baby securely when bouncing him.

■ The following is a traditional bouncing rhyme to try:

To market, to market, to buy a fat pig.
Home again, home again, jiggity jig.
To market, to market, to buy a plum bun.
Home again, home again, market is done.

48

WHAT BRAIN RESEARCH SAYS

Dramatic speech encourages emotional expression in babies. This in turn activates the brain to release chemicals that help memory.

Choo Choo Train

■ As you say the following rhyme, move your fingers up your baby's arm and back down again:

> Choo choo train, choo choo train
> Going up the track.
> Toot, toot, toot, toot
> Now it's coming back.

■ Repeat for the other arm.

■ Be dramatic with the word "toot" and soon your baby will be trying to make that sound.

Swinging

49

WHAT BRAIN RESEARCH SAYS

Infants possess an abundance of genes and brain synapses that immediately make them ready for learning music.

- The action of a swing is very appealing to an infant.

- If you say poems or sing songs as you swing your baby, he will develop a sense of rhythm as well as some very important brain connections.

- Sit your baby in your lap as you swing back and forth. Say the following poem as you swing:

> *Back and forth, back and forth*
> *Swinging, swinging*
> *Back and forth*

- Another good poem to say is "The Swing" by Robert Louis Stevenson.

**WHAT BRAIN
RESEARCH SAYS**

Wiggles and
scoots help the
formation of the
brain synapses
that develop
future large
motor skills.

Wiggles and Scoots

- Babies wiggle themselves all over the place. These wiggles and scoots are preparing them to crawl.

- Place your baby on his tummy and lay on the floor facing him.

- Put an interesting toy in front of him but just out of his reach.

- Move the toy (balls with jingles are good) back and forth.

- As he attempts to get the ball, he will probably scoot forward a little.

- Give him a chance to retrieve the ball and praise him generously.

- This kind of success develops great self-confidence.

Push the Baby

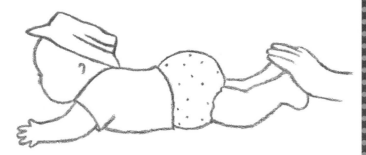

WHAT BRAIN RESEARCH SAYS

Work on both small and large motor skills at the same time since they develop independently.

■ Lay your baby on his stomach.

■ Get behind your baby and put your hands on the soles of his feet.

■ When he feels your hands, he will try to bring himself forward by pushing on your hands.

■ This is a preparation exercise for crawling.

■ Sometimes he will need a gentle push from you.

■ While lightly pushing his feet, say the following poem:

Take your little feet and push, push, push. (gently push)
Take your little feet and push, push, push. (gently push)
Take your little feet and push, push, push. (gently push)
Push, push, all day long.

52

**WHAT BRAIN
RESEARCH SAYS**

Repeating a
motor skill over
and over will
develop neural
circuits that move
from the brain's
thinking areas into
the motor cortex
and out to the
nerves that move
the muscles.

Changing Hands

■ During this time period, your baby may begin to transfer an object from one hand to his other hand.

■ You can help strengthen the neural circuits in the brain by helping him practice changing hands. This game develops small motor skills and eye-hand coordination.

■ Put a small rattle into one of his hands.

■ Shake his hand with the rattle.

■ Show him how to transfer the rattle to his other hand. These are the steps.

✓ Put his empty hand on the rattle and he will automatically grab it.

✓ Undo his fingers on the first hand, then kiss his fingers.

Pretty Light

WHAT BRAIN RESEARCH SAYS

When an infant looks at moving objects, a neuron from his retina makes a connection to another neuron in the visual part of his brain. He is literally "wiring" his vision.

- If desired, cover a flashlight with colored plastic wrap.

- Hold your baby in your arms and turn on the flashlight.

- Slowly move it back and forth and watch as he follows the light.

- Talk to him as you move the light.

> Pretty light,
> Pretty light,
> See the pretty, pretty, light.

- Not only do babies love to do this, while they are having fun they are making important connections in the brain.

Where's the Toy?

- Hold a favorite toy in front of your baby and then put it out of sight.

- Encourage him to look for the toy. Ask questions like, "Is it in the sky?", then look up to the sky.

- Ask, "Is it on the ground?", then look down to the ground.

- Ask, "Is it in my hands?" Yes, here it is.

- As your baby develops, he will begin to look for the toy when you remove it from his sight.

- Once he has started to pay attention to where the toy went, he will follow your movements as you put it out of sight.

6 to 9 Months

**WHAT BRAIN
RESEARCH SAYS**

Since the
neurons for
vision begin to
form very early,
babies need
stimulating
visual experi-
ences.

Mirror Games

■ It seems that the more a baby sees, the more she wants to
see.

■ Looking into a mirror is great fun and gives your baby
another perspective on who she is.

■ Here are some things that you can do with your baby as
you look into a full-length mirror.

✓ Smile.

✓ Shake different parts of the body.

✓ Make faces with silly sounds.

✓ Make sounds with your lips.

✓ Make animal sounds.

✓ Rock back and forth.

Sounds Everywhere

WHAT BRAIN RESEARCH SAYS

Babies hearts beat faster when their parents make eye contact and speak in a melodious voice.

■ Expose your baby to a variety of sounds.

■ Make sounds with your mouth and put your baby's fingers on your mouth as you make the sounds.

✓ Buzz like a bee.

✓ Hum.

✓ Pop your cheeks.

✓ Make a siren sound.

✓ Cough.

✓ Pretend to sneeze.

■ Crunch different kinds of paper. Cellophane and tissue paper have interesting sounds.

**WHAT BRAIN
RESEARCH SAYS**

Musical experiences enhance the future ability to reason abstractly, particularly in the spatial domains.

Where Is the Sound?

- Auditory awareness is something that comes with age and experience.

- Playing games to heighten your baby's hearing awareness will help wire her brain.

- Take a wind-up musical toy and put it out of your baby's sight.

- Wind it up and ask her, "Where's the music?"

- When she turns to the sound, praise her generously.

- Repeat this game in different parts of the room.

- If your baby is crawling, you can hide the music under a pillow or elsewhere so that she can crawl to the music.

Playing With Pots

WHAT BRAIN RESEARCH SAYS

Positive early experiences determine how the intricate neural circuits of the brain are "wired."

- Playing with pots is a good way to teach your baby many things.

- Put a pot face down on the floor with a toy under it.

- Say "one, two, three, diddely dee" and lift the pot off the hidden toy.

- Your baby will be delighted and want you to do it again and again.

- Now hide the toy and help your baby lift the pot up.

- The next step is to turn the pot over. Show your baby how to do this and then help him try.

- When you turn the pot right side up, take the same toy and drop it into the pot.

**WHAT BRAIN
RESEARCH SAYS**

Using small
motor muscles
stimulates brain
growth.

Rum Tum Tum

■ Babies love to hold things in their hands and hit them on a
surface. This is excellent for motor coordination and lots of
fun, too.

■ Give your baby a wooden spoon and encourage him to
bang it on the floor.

■ Sing a variety of your favorite songs as you both bang the
spoons.

■ Try banging spoons to the following poem:

Rum, tum, tum
Rum, tum, tum
Bang the drum
Rum, tum, tum

Baby Shakers

WHAT BRAIN RESEARCH SAYS

Dr. Edwin Gordon, an authority in music learning theory, confirms that infants possess an abundance of genes and synapses that immediately make them ready for learning music.

■ Put some buttons in a metal container. Tape the top carefully so that your baby cannot get it open.

■ Shake the container and listen to the noise. Watch your baby's eyes grow big with excitement.

■ Give the shaker to your baby and let her shake it as you sing your favorite songs.

■ Try singing "Old MacDonald Had a Farm," shaking and making animal sounds together. What could be more fun for a baby!

■ You can also turn a see-through plastic bottle into a shaker. Your little one will enjoy watching the rocks or buttons move when they are being shaken.

■ A set of measuring spoons also makes a good shaker.

61

Babies need touching experi-ences to "grow" the brain and grow the brain and the body. They are as critical as nutrients and vitamins.

One, Two

■ Make up rhymes as you hold your baby's hand and let him touch different parts of your body.

■ Here are some ideas:

> *One, two, touch my shoe.*
> *Yellow, red, touch my head.*
> *Dippity dips, touch my lips.*
> *Apples, pear, touch my hair.*

■ Each time you say the body part, put your child's hand on that part. When you say, "One, two, touch my shoe," put his hand on your shoe.

■ Reverse the game and touch your baby as you say the rhyme.

Tommy Thumb

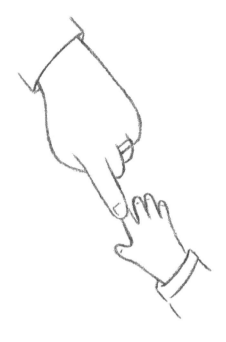

WHAT BRAIN RESEARCH SAYS

The language development opportunities of songs and fingerplays are vital in the development of the brain.

■ Say the rhyme as you touch your baby's fingers one by one.

■ On the final verse, wave your baby's hand.

Tommy thumb, Tommy thumb,
Where are you?
Here I am, here I am.
How do you do!

■ Repeat with Peter pointer, Toby tall, Ruby ring, Sally small, and fingers all.

■ Your baby will respond to your touch and your voice.

Playing Ball

WHAT BRAIN RESEARCH SAYS

Each young brain forms the neuronal and muscular connections required for sitting, crawling, walking, and talking at its own pace.

- As soon as your baby can sit up easily, try rolling a ball to her.

- A soft, cloth ball is good to start with.

- Roll the ball gently and show her how to catch it.

- Babies love this game and get very excited when the ball is coming toward them.

- Sing a song to the tune of "Row, Row, Row Your Boat" as you roll the ball.

   Roll, roll, roll the ball
   To my baby dear
   Rolling, rolling, rolling, rolling,
   To my baby dear.

- This game develops motor dexterity.

This Is the Way

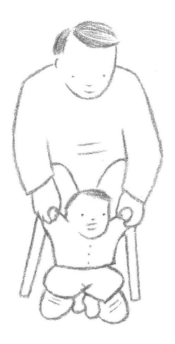

64

WHAT BRAIN RESEARCH SAYS

A nurturing environment can build pathways that encourage emotional strength, while repeated exposure to stress can create brain connections that trigger fear.

■ Sit on a chair with a straight back. Cross your legs and sit your baby on your ankles.

■ Hold her hands as you move your legs up and down.

■ Sing your favorite songs as you bounce up and down, or sing the following to the tune of "This Is the Way":

> *This is the way we bounce, bounce, bounce*
> *Up and down, up and down.*
> *This is the way we bounce, bounce, bounce*
> *Every single morning.*
> *Wheeeee (hold your legs up for two seconds and then lower them)*

65

Babies who are cuddled and cared for—who aren't spoiled but have their emotional needs met—are more likely to demonstrate caring behavior later.

Little Cheek

■ Touching your baby as you speak to him develops trust between the two of you.

■ Say the following rhyme to your baby:

Little cheek, (touch his cheek)
Little chin, (touch his chin)
Here is where the food comes in. (touch his mouth)
Little eyes, (touch his eyes)
Little nose, (touch his nose)
Now I'll kiss your little toes. (kiss your baby's toes)
by Jackie Silberg

■ This rhyme is excellent for language development as well as bonding.

Puppet Peekaboo

WHAT BRAIN RESEARCH SAYS

With every game of peekaboo, thousands of connections among brain cells are formed or strengthened, adding a bit more development to the complex "wiring" that will remain largely in place for the rest of the child's life. These connections are more difficult to make later on.

Children love watching and playing with puppets.

Put a puppet on your hand and hold it behind your back.

Bring out the puppet and say, "Peekaboo, (child's name)."

Now put it behind your back again.

Continue doing this until your baby begins to anticipate the puppet coming out at a certain place.

Then bring the puppet out at a different place—over your head, over the baby's head. Always bring it down in front of your baby's face (not too close) when you say the peekaboo words.

Give the puppet to your baby and see if she will imitate you.

**WHAT BRAIN
RESEARCH SAYS**

Peekaboo
games teach
babies that
objects that
disappear will
come back
again. A strong,
secure connec-
tion with your
child helps him
withstand the
ordinary stresses
of daily life.

Whoops

- Sit your baby on the floor or in a chair facing you.

- Take a towel and put it over your face.

- Say the words "peekaboo" as you take the towel off and show your face to your baby.

- This game usually brings forth gales of laughter and the more you do it, the funnier it becomes.

- Try putting the towel on your baby's head and pulling it off.

- Try putting the towel on your baby's head and see if she will pull it off.

- Remember to say "peekaboo" each time you take off the towel.

Where's the Ball?

WHAT BRAIN RESEARCH SAYS

A study at the University of Alabama found that blocks, beads, peekaboo, and other "old-fashioned" measures strengthened cognitive, motor, and language development.

- Lay on the floor with your baby.

- Hold a small ball (or other toy) in your hand and talk about it with your baby.

- Put the ball out of the baby's sight—behind a chair, in your pocket, etc.

- Ask the baby, "Where's the ball?"

- Take out the ball and say "peekaboo."

- Continue playing the game and change the location of the ball each time.

WHAT BRAIN RESEARCH SAYS

Games like peekaboo are the building blocks of language and teach babies about face-to-face communication.

Noisy Peekaboo

- Sit your baby in a chair facing you.

- Hold a large towel in front of your face.

- Count out loud "one, two, three."

- On "three" move the towel away from your face and make a silly sound.

- Some sounds you could make are:
  - ✓ goo, goo, goo
  - ✓ tongue clicks
  - ✓ pops

- Your baby will laugh a lot. This is really a lot of fun.

Baby, Baby—A Peekaboo Game

WHAT BRAIN RESEARCH SAYS

Talking to a child from an early age will help that child to learn to speak.

■ Say the following rhyme and do the actions:

Baby, baby, rock in the cradle. (rock your baby)

Baby, baby, jump in the bed. (put your baby down on her back)

Baby, baby, smile at your daddy. (hold your face close to your baby's face and smile)

Baby, baby, wiggle your head. (hold your baby's head and gently move it from side to side)

Baby, baby, play hide and seek. (put your hands over your eyes)

Baby, baby, shall we peek? (take your hands away from your eyes)

Baby, baby, what do you see? (bring your face close to your baby's face)

I am back, yes, sireeeee! (give your baby a nice hug)

by Jackie Silberg

71

Although pat-a-
cake and peeka-
boo look like
innocent play,
these games
communicate
complex sets of
rules about turn-
taking and
expectations.

Peekaboo Fun

- There are so many different kinds of peekaboo games, and babies love them all.

- The favorite is covering your face with your hands and then taking them away.

- This method of peekaboo shows your baby that even though she can't see your face, you are still there.

- This game is very important in wiring the brain. Your baby will grow intellectually with this game.

- Other ways to play peekaboo:

  ✓ Put your baby's hands over his eyes and take them away.

  ✓ Hold a diaper between you and your child. Peek out of the side and the top of the diaper.

  ✓ Toss the diaper over your head and then take it away.

Peekaboo Music

WHAT BRAIN RESEARCH SAYS

Brain cells make new connections and strengthen existing ones with peekaboo games.

■ Sing this song to the tune of "Are You Sleeping":

Are you sleeping, are you sleeping
Little (child's name), little (child's name)?
Now it's time to wake up,
Now it's time to wake up,
Ding, ding, dong
Ding, ding, dong.

■ Use this as a peekaboo song.

■ Cover your eyes as you sing "are you sleeping?"

■ When you sing "now it's time to wake up," take your baby's hands and gently pull her upward.

■ When you sing "ding, ding, dong," move your baby's hands up and down as if she is ringing a bell.

WHAT BRAIN RESEARCH SAYS

Interactive games with babies prepare them for more intricate relationships later in life.

Where Am I?

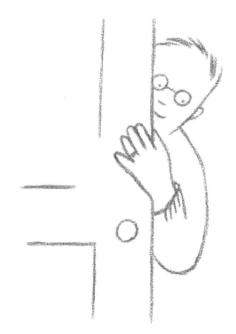

- When babies learn to be aware of their environment, their visual skills will constantly improve.

- Play a hiding game with your baby.

- Partially hide yourself from your baby behind a chair or a door. Always let part of yourself show.

- Say the following poem to your little one:

  Where am I? Where am I?

  Can you find me, can you find me?

  Where am I? Where am I?

  Oops, here I am.

- When you say the last line, if your baby has not found you, show yourself.

- The joy that you will see on your baby's face when she finds you will make you want to play this game many, many times.

The Big Squeeze

WHAT BRAIN RESEARCH SAYS

Exercising small muscles has a positive effect on the motor areas of the brain.

- Squeeze toys are great fun to play with. The rubbery kind seem to be the easiest to squeeze.

- Your baby is developing her small motor skills when she squeezes things.

- If she is having trouble, put your hands over hers and squeeze the toy. Once she gets the feeling in her hands, she will be able to do it herself.

- Here is a fun little poem to say as you squeeze the toy:

> *Squeeze the cheese, Louise, please!*
> *Squeeze the cheese, Louise, please!*
> *Not the bees and not the trees*
> *Squeeze the cheese, Louise, please!*

75

Little Stuff

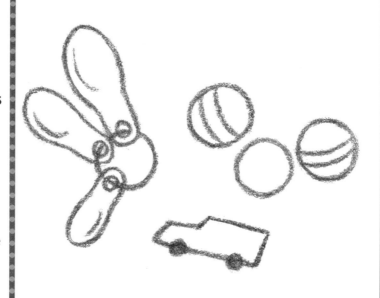

WHAT BRAIN RESEARCH SAYS

Small and large motor skills develop separately. Even though they require the same physical foundations, the two skills advance a little bit at a time.

- You can enhance your baby's small motor skills by doing activities with her.

- Give your little one a variety of small and safe objects to play with. Start with measuring spoons, small balls, and small toys.

- Put an object in your baby's hand and encourage her to drop it.

- Give her a container to drop her treasures in and then watch her take the treasures out.

- Encourage her to give you an object and then be sure to give it back.

- See if she can hold two things in the same hand. This might be a little hard.

Touching Textures

WHAT BRAIN RESEARCH SAYS

Through interaction, babies develop the network of brain cells that helps them learn to calm themselves.

- Games that encourage eye-hand coordination are important to play with your baby because they help develop the wiring in her brain.

- Gather together strips of different kinds of materials—wool, cotton, velvet, satin, and any others that you might have.

- Sit on the floor with your baby and hold out one of the material pieces close enough for her to reach. When she grabs at it, praise her.

- Once she has touched the strip of material, tell her the name of it and place it on her palm. Describe the feel of the material. "This is velvet and it feels smooth."

- She will not understand all of your words, but she will associate the sound of your voice with the feel of the material.

77

**WHAT BRAIN
RESEARCH SAYS**

Practice in eye-
hand coordina-
tion will develop
"wiring" in the
brain.

Peas and Carrots

■ Babies enjoy eating with their fingers. In fact, it's an important step in developing small motor skills.

■ When babies can pick up food and put it in their mouths,
they have a strong feeling of power and control that makes
them feel wonderful.

■ Put some cooked peas and carrots on the table in front of
your baby.

■ Sing the following song to the tune of "Frere Jacques":

Peas and carrots, peas and carrots

Here they are, here they are.

Put them in your mouth, put them in your mouth.

Yum, yum, yum

Yum, yum, yum

■ Guide the little fingers to the peas and carrots and then to
her mouth. She will probably want to feed you, too!

Another Pop Game

WHAT BRAIN RESEARCH SAYS

Holding and stroking a baby stimulates the brain to release important hormones that allow her to grow.

- Movement and music together stimulate both sides of the brain.

- Hold your baby in your arms as you move around the room and sing "Pop Goes the Weasel."

- When you come to the word "pop," hold your baby high into the air, then bring her down for a kiss.

All around the cobblers bench
The monkey chased the weasel.
The monkey laughed to see such sport
Pop! goes the baby. (or say your child's name)

Sing and Say

WHAT BRAIN RESEARCH SAYS

The earlier music is introduced, the more potential a child has for learning. Children surrounded by words almost always become fluent by three years old. Children deprived of language experiences rarely master language as adults.

■ In a study reported in Newsweek (2-19-96), researchers at the University of Konstanz in Germany found that "exposure to music rewires neural circuits in the brain."

■ Think of some of your favorite songs and sing them to your baby.

■ Whatever songs you sing, your baby is going to enjoy hearing the words. It doesn't matter that she doesn't understand them.

■ If your song has a familiar word that you know your little one understands, sing that word louder than the others.

■ Instead of singing, try saying the same words in different ways—whisper, soft, loud, and high-pitched.

■ Whether you sing or speak the words, the rhythm will open windows of opportunity in your child's brain.

Sing About the Day

WHAT BRAIN RESEARCH SAYS

Songs introduce babies to speech patterns and sensory motor skills.

- The more words your baby hears, the more those parts of the brain will develop.

- Review your day in song. Make up any melody and sing about what you did that particular day.

- Sing about waking up, getting dressed, eating breakfast, riding in the car, etc.

- You can also sing about people in your baby's life.

- Sing about grandparents: "Grandma loves you and gives you a kiss."

- Sing about brothers and sisters: "Sister Sue loves you, you, you."

- Sing about pets.

- These musical "conversations" will give your baby a basis for learning.

Soothing Singing

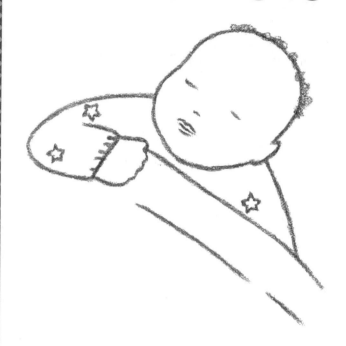

WHAT BRAIN RESEARCH SAYS

Infants and their parents are biologically wired to have close emotional ties, which develop slowly over the baby's first year of life with coos, gazes, and smiles.

■ You don't have to be a great singer to sing to your baby. The softness of your voice calms a baby and establishes a wonderful bond between the two of you.

■ Make up a melody to this old Russian lullaby or say these words as you rock your baby:

> *Go to sleep my darling baby.*
> *Babushka baio*
> *See the moon is shining on you.*
> *Babushka baio*
> *I will tell you many stories,*
> *If you close your eyes.*
> *Go to sleep my darling baby.*
> *Babushka baio*

A Goodnight Rhyme

WHAT BRAIN RESEARCH SAYS

Holding and cuddling comforts your baby and helps his brain grow.

■ Rock your baby as you say the following rhyme:

> *Good night sweet baby, goodnight sweet one,*
> *The clock is ticking and says "were done."*
> *Goodnight sweet baby, goodnight my dear*
> *The stars are twinkling and sleep is near.*

■ Gently put your baby in his bed and say "Good night, good night."

■ Rub his back and give him a kiss.

Love Those Keys!

**WHAT BRAIN
RESEARCH SAYS**

Exercising
small muscles
stimulates brain
development.

- Keys are a favorite toy for babies. They make noise and are easy to hold, and babies like to drop them.

- Hold the keys in your hand and say "One, two, three, let's drop the keys."

- Drop the keys on the floor and be sure your little one watches them drop.

- Put the keys in your baby's hand and repeat.

- Open your babies fingers and let the keys drop.

- After a few times, your baby will know what to do and will delight in this game.

- This is an excellent game for developing small motor skills.

Waving

■ Wave your baby's feet and hands to people or pets your baby knows.

■ It's best to play the game when the actual people are in the room.

■ Sing the song to the tune of "Frere Jacques":

> *Wave to daddy, wave to daddy*
>
> *Wave, wave, wave*
>
> *Wave, wave, wave*
>
> *Say hello to daddy, say hello to daddy*
>
> *Wave, wave, wave*
>
> *Wave, wave, wave*

■ You can wave with either hands or feet to mommy, grandma, grandpa, friends, and pets.

Gurgle, Gurgle, Squish

WHAT BRAIN RESEARCH SAYS

Every new motor skill has to be repeated over and over to strengthen the neural circuits.

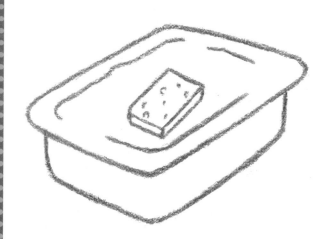

This is a good game to play outside with a baby pool or a large container of water.

Put some sponges in the water and show your baby how to squeeze the water out of the sponge.

Squeeze the water on your hands, your arms, and other parts of the body.

Now give your baby some plastic cups and show her how to squeeze the water into the cups.

This game will occupy your baby for a long time, and it's great for developing small motor skills.

Play a game by saying silly words as you squeeze. Here are a few ideas:

✓ Swish ✓ Gurgle ✓ Squish ✓ Oo, oo, oo

Listening Fun

■ The more experience that your little one has listening, the better language she will have.

■ Include your baby as much as you can in family conversations. At the dinner table, listening to others talk will teach her numerous words.

■ Remember that even though your baby cannot say the words, she still understands them.

■ Listen to the radio and vary the programs. Music and news will let her hear many different sounding voices.

■ Many times he will respond to what he is hearing. Try to encourage her responses and interact with her.

87

**WHAT BRAIN
RESEARCH SAYS**

Acquiring a set
of sounds is a
first step toward
language, but
just a baby step.
To start decod-
ing speech, you
have to recog-
nize words.

Reading Tips

■ Set aside a special time each day for books. Bedtime often
works well.

■ Select books with short sentences and simple illustrations.

■ Let your baby hold the book and turn the pages.

■ Just name the pictures. The story will come later.

■ Stop and talk about anything that your baby seems interested in. A picture may remind her of something else. Keep
the conversation going and use lots of descriptive words.

■ Most importantly: repeat, repeat, repeat. Your baby will
want to read the same book over and over. The more you
repeat, the more the brain gets wired.

Let's Climb

WHAT BRAIN RESEARCH SAYS

Each young brain forms, at its own pace, the neural and muscular connections required for crawling and climbing.

■ There is no avoiding it! Your baby will begin to climb everything in sight. Why not help her along and develop her large motor muscles?

■ Take cushions and pillows and pile them on the floor.

■ Put your baby in front of the pillows and she will have a wonderful time.

■ Take a favorite toy and put it on top of one of the pillows. This will entice her even more.

The Signing Game

WHAT BRAIN RESEARCH SAYS

The brain is capable of learning throughout life, but no other time will ever equal this most profuse time of learning.

- Much research has been done about teaching sign language to babies.

- For example, if you are reading a book to your baby and there is a picture of a cat, you can say the word and do the sign. This helps her make the connection between the word and the picture.

- Here are three simple signs to teach your baby:

  ✓ Cat—take the palm of your hand and stroke the back of your other hand.

  ✓ Fish—open and close your mouth like a fish.

  ✓ Bird—flap your arms up and down in the air.

- Singing songs that use these words is an excellent way to reinforce the signs. A song like "Old MacDonald" is a good one to sing.

9 to 12 Months

90

WHAT BRAIN RESEARCH SAYS

Early childhood experiences exert a dramatic and precise impact, physically determining how the intricate neural circuits of the brain are wired.

Outside Exploring

- Playing outside on a lovely day is a wonderful way to experience all of the senses.

- Let your baby crawl in the grass while you crawl along with him.

- Name each thing that your baby seems interested in.

- Smell flowers, tickle with grass, look for bugs, etc. There are so many things to do.

- Rolling over in the grass is fun to do and your baby will enjoy the light, prickly feel of it.

Seek and Ye Shall Find

91

WHAT BRAIN RESEARCH SAYS

An infant's brain can discern every possible sound in every language. By ten months, babies have learned to screen out foreign sounds and to focus on the sounds of their native language.

- Listening for the source of a sound is a very good game to develop auditory awareness.

- These games need to be played in the early years to strengthen brain connections for the future.

- You will need a wind-up clock that makes a nice sound.

- Hold the clock and sing a little tick, tock song with your baby.
  > *Tick, tock, tick tock*
  > *Goes the clock,*
  > *Tick, tock*

- Now take the clock and put it under a pillow.

- Ask your little one, "Where is the tick tock?"

- Help guide him to the clock, using the sound to locate it. Once he understands how to play this game, he will want to do it again and again.

In and Out

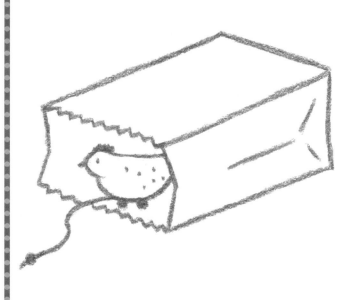

WHAT BRAIN RESEARCH SAYS

Early experiences shape the way circuits are made in the brain.

Understanding spatial concepts like *in, out, over, under,* and *behind* are important for brain development.

Playing games that encourage this understanding will benefit your baby in future years.

Start with inside and outside.

Take a large paper sack—the kind that your cat would like—and put a favorite toy inside.

Help your baby find the toy and take it out.

Put it back in again and keep playing the game over and over.

Make up a silly song, such as the one below, and say it each time you put the toy back into the sack.

Sacky, wacky, toysie, woysie

Boom, boom, boom (say the last boom in a bigger voice)

Where Is...?

WHAT BRAIN RESEARCH SAYS

A warm, loving relationship with a baby strengthens the biological systems that help him handle emotions.

- Sit down with your baby and look at pictures together.

- Find a picture of someone in your family.

- Talk about the picture by naming the person in it. Say the name again and ask your baby to point to the person in the picture.

- Now, cover up the picture with your hand and ask your baby to find the person.

- Continue playing this game with another picture.

- Your baby might surprise you by how much he understands!

Where's the Baby?

WHAT BRAIN RESEARCH SAYS

Researchers now confirm that how you interact with your baby and the experiences you provide have an impact on his emotional development and learning abilities.

- Find several pictures of a baby and hide them in different places.

- Choose places that are familiar to your baby—in the toy box, on the ceiling above the changing place, or under a plate on the highchair.

- Say, "Let's go find the baby."

- Ask different questions: "Is it in the sink?" "Is it on the chair?"

- Finally ask the question, "Is it in the toy box (or other place)?"

- When your baby finds the picture, praise him and clap your hands.

- You can play this game with pictures of family members and friends.

I Touch

WHAT BRAIN RESEARCH SAYS

Touching babies helps their digestion and relieves stress.

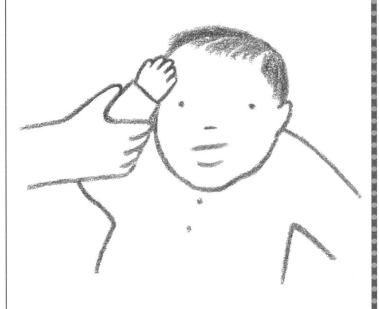

■ This rhyme helps your baby identify his body parts.

■ First say the rhyme and point to each part of your body.

■ Next, take your baby's hand and point to each part of his body as you say the following rhyme:

> *I'll touch my chin, my cheek, my chair.*
> *I'll touch my head, my heels, my hair.*
> *I'll touch my knees, my neck, my nose.*
> *Then I'll bend and touch my toes.*

■ You are also saying words that begin with the same sound.

Father, Mother, and Uncle John

WHAT BRAIN RESEARCH SAYS

A strong emotional bond with a baby actually affects the baby's biological systems that adapt to stress.

- Put your infant on your lap facing you and recite the following rhyme as you bounce your knees.

- On the words "father fell off," hold your baby tightly and pretend to fall to one side.

- On the words "mother fell off," again holding your baby tightly, pretend to fall to the other side.

    Father, mother, and Uncle John
    Rode to the doctor one by one
    Father fell off
    Mother fell off
    But Uncle John rode on and on
    Father fell off
    Mother fell off
    But Uncle John rode on

This Is Bill

■ Sit your baby on your lap

■ Hold one ankle in each hand as you say the following rhyme:

This is Bill and this is Jill.
They went out to play.
Over and over, (move his legs over each other)
Over and over, (move his legs over in the other direction)
"This is fun," said Bill and Jill.
And they said, "Hooray!" (give your baby a big hug)

98

WHAT BRAIN RESEARCH SAYS

Sensory experiences and social interactions with infants will boost their future intellectual abilities.

Wash the Toy

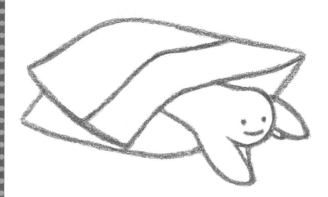

- Wet washcloths are wonderful fun for babies. The texture feels good all over his body and especially on his face.

- Play peekaboo with a washcloth when giving him a bath.

- Tuck a small toy in a washcloth and let your little one put his fingers in the folds to find the toy.

- Give your baby the washcloth and let him wash your face.

- Sing the following to the tune, "Row, Row, Row Your Boat":

    Wash, wash, wash the ball.

    Get it nice and clean.

    Scrubby, scrubby, scrubby, scrubby, (move child's hand over the ball with the washcloth)

    Now it's nice and clean.

Bathtub Hickory

WHAT BRAIN RESEARCH SAYS

Language skills and future language capacity develops best in an environment rich in spoken language.

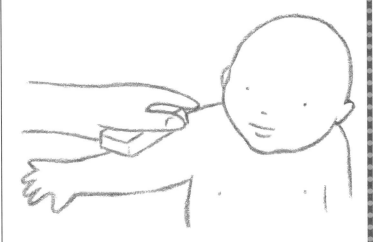

■ Hickory, Dickory, Dock is a wonderful nursery rhyme to sing and play when giving your baby a bath.

> *Hickory, Dickory, Dock,*
> *The mouse ran up the clock.*
> *The clock struck one and down he did run,*
> *Hickory, Dickory, Dock.*

■ Take the soap or the washcloth and slowly move up your baby's arm as you sing "the mouse ran up the clock."

■ On the words "down he did run," slide the washcloth down your baby's arm and make a splash in the water.

■ You can also play this game by moving a toy up and down the side of the bathtub.

100

WHAT BRAIN RESEARCH SAYS

Scientists are just now realizing how experiences after birth determine the actual "wiring" of the human brain.

Falling Ice

- This is a great bathtub game.

- Fill a cup with ice cubes.

- Give your child another cup.

- Drop an ice cube in the tub and see if your baby can retrieve it with his cup.

- This is a lot of fun because he will have to chase it around the water with his cup.

- If he is having trouble, show him how to retrieve the ice cube.

- Another fun game with ice cubes is to put one ice cube in your baby's hand and show him how to drop it into the water and then catch it with the cup.

Row, Row, Your Boat

WHAT BRAIN RESEARCH SAYS

Babies who don't get their quota of tender loving care (TLC) early in life may lack the proper brain "wiring" to form close relationships.

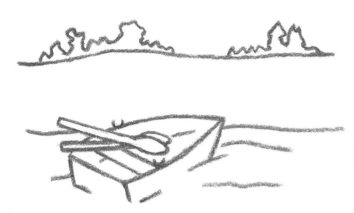

■ This is a bathtub game that develops trust between you and your child.

■ While sitting in the bathtub, hold your baby firmly and guide him back and forth in the water like a boat.

■ As you are moving your baby through the water, sing the following song:

> *Row, row, row your boat*
> *Gently down the stream.*
> *Merrily, merrily, merrily, merrily*
> *Life is but a dream. Splash! (splash the water)*

■ Sing other water songs as you play the game. "Sailing, Sailing," "It's Raining It's Pouring," and "Rain, Rain, Go Away" are a few good water songs.

102

WHAT BRAIN RESEARCH SAYS

Using muscles repeatedly gives them the power and pliability known as "muscle tone," which is important in developing the nervous system.

One, Two, Three, Kick

■ Show your little one how you hold on to the side of a chair and kick your leg in the air.

■ Encourage him to copy you.

■ Say, "One, two, three, kick" and kick your leg in the air on the word "kick."

■ Listening for the word "kick" is a lot of fun for babies and kicking a leg into the air develops muscle strength.

■ Kick in front, kick to the side, and kick in back.

■ Try counting in a soft voice and saying the word "kick" in a big voice.

La-Di-Da

WHAT BRAIN RESEARCH SAYS

The connections neurons make with one another are called synapses. While various parts of the brain develop at different rates, study after study has shown that the peak production period for synapses is from birth to the later elementary school years.

- This is both a good stretching exercise and a great way to learn the names of body parts.

- Lift your arms high in the air and then bend down and try to touch your toes.

- Encourage your baby to do the same.

- As you lift your arms in the air, say:

    Up high in the air

    Down low to the toes

    La di da, la di da, la di da.

- Do this several times and then try naming another part of the body. For example, say:

    Up high in the air

    Down to the knees

    La di da, la di da, la di da

- Your baby will enjoy saying the words "la di da."

104

A strong secure attachment to a nurturing adult can have a protective biological function, helping a growing child withstand the stresses of daily life.

Rolling

■ Show your baby how to make a fist.

■ Take his fists and roll them over each other.

■ As you roll them, say the following rhyme:

> *Rolling, rolling, little hands,*
> *Rolling down the street.*
> *Rolling slowly, (roll her hands slowly)*
> *Getting faster, (pick up the speed)*
> *Roll, roll, roll, roll, roll. (roll faster and faster)*

■ End with a big hug and kiss.

Silly Antics

105

WHAT BRAIN RESEARCH SAYS

Expressing emotions activates chemicals in the brain that heighten memory.

- Developing an awareness of the world is something that you can do with your baby.

- Sit on the floor with your baby facing you.

- Do a variety of silly things and encourage him to imitate you. Here are some ideas:

  ✓ Make a funny face.

  ✓ Stick out your tongue and make silly sounds.

  ✓ Move your head in different directions, up and down and side to side.

  ✓ Pound your fists on your chest and yell.

  ✓ Make different animal sounds.

  ✓ Lie on your back and kick your legs in the air.

  ✓ Get on your hands and knees and bark like a dog.

- After you have done several of these, repeat them in front of a mirror. When your baby sees himself doing the antics, he'll have even more fun and develop an additional awareness.

WHAT BRAIN RESEARCH SAYS

Helping a baby's brain "grow" means immersing him in environments that are emotionally and intellectually rich and stimulating.

What Can You Do With a Stacking Toy?

- Stacking toys have lots of possibilities for developmental play.

- Depending on your baby's developmental needs and skills, encourage him to try any of the following:

  ✓ Stacking them large to small, small to large, and any old way.

  ✓ Throwing the rings.

  ✓ Putting the rings on his fingers.

  ✓ Putting the rings in his mouth.

  ✓ Spinning the rings.

- All toys have great creative possibilities. Help your baby see the different ways to play with toys.

Piggyback

WHAT BRAIN RESEARCH SAYS

Touching, patting, and hugging babies increases their ability to digest food more easily.

■ If your baby enjoys piggyback rides, this game is great fun.

■ Your baby should sit on your shoulders with his legs dangling down in front (or on your back with his hands around your neck).

■ Hold on to his hands as you move about. Say the following:

>*Walking, walking, all around the room.*
>*Faster, faster, all around the room.*

■ Try different movements as you take your child for a piggy-back ride—hop, skip, march, turn in a circle, go slowly, go fast, and so on.

■ Piggyback rides help strengthen balancing skills.

108

WHAT BRAIN
RESEARCH SAYS

Songs, move-
ment, and
musical games
of childhood
have been
called "brilliant
neurological
exercises" that
introduce
children to
speech patterns,
sensory motor
skills, and essen-
tial movement
skills.

Humpty Dumpty

■ Say the popular nursery rhyme as you bounce your baby
on your knees.

Humpty Dumpty sat on a wall. (bounce baby)

*Humpty Dumpty had a great fall. (open your knees and,
while holding your baby securely, let him slide down to
the ground)*

All the kings horses and all the kings men

*Couldn't put Humpty together again. (bring baby back to
your knees)*

■ Give your baby a favorite stuffed animal to hold as you
play this game.

■ This may give him the idea to play the game with his
stuffed animal.

Chin to Chin

WHAT BRAIN RESEARCH SAYS

Most of a child's brain development takes place after birth. The experiences he has will shape the developing structure of his brain.

- Put your baby on his back and touch his chin.

- Say the word "chin" and touch your chin.

- Put your chin on your baby's chin and say the word again.

- Keep repeating this activity with different parts of your body touching the same parts of your baby's body.

- Face, nose, cheek, and head are good ones to start with.

- Helping your baby realize that he has the same body parts as you do will increase his awareness of his surroundings.

110

WHAT BRAIN RESEARCH SAYS

Most scientists now agree that motor development occurs when the brain has been "wired" for the task, like finches or sparrows, who learn to sing as hatchlings or not at all.

Copy Me

- Developing large motor skills will help babies make brain connections.

- Do an action and ask your child to copy you. If he doesn't understand what "copy me" means, move his body to copy what you do.

- Try looking in a full-length mirror as you play this game.

- Here are some actions that you can do:
  - ✓ Take giant steps—if your child isn't walking, do it crawling.
  - ✓ Take little steps—if your child isn't walking, do it crawling.
  - ✓ Hold one arm out to the side and make big circles.
  - ✓ Make circles with the other arm.
  - ✓ Hold a large beach ball, then drop it and pick it up.

Let's Pull

111

WHAT BRAIN RESEARCH SAYS

With muscles and coordination working together, babies can begin to develop more demanding skills, like walking.

- This game develops upper arm strength, and your baby will absolutely adore it.

- Sit on the floor facing your baby.

- Take one end of a long scarf and give the other end to your baby.

- Start gently pulling the scarf and show your baby how to pull back.

- When he begins to pull hard, fall over. This is always hilarious to babies.

- This game is excellent for muscle development and lots of fun to play.

112

WHAT BRAIN RESEARCH SAYS

Early music experiences increase and enhance spatial-temporal reasoning and the learning of mathematical concepts.

Fast and Slow Rhythms

- Give your baby some wooden spoons or rhythm sticks.

- Put him in a highchair or have him sit on the floor or other place that has a nice surface for hitting the sticks.

- You should have some wooden spoons or rhythm sticks, too.

- Sing a song like "The Wheels on the Bus" and hit the sticks to the beat of the song.

- Encourage your baby to hit his sticks, too.

- Sing the same song faster and hit your sticks faster.

- Sing the song slowly and hit your sticks slowly.

- Your baby will enjoy watching you hit the sticks faster and slower. He will begin to understand fast and slow.

Mouth Songs

WHAT BRAIN RESEARCH SAYS

Songs, movement, and musical games of childhood are neurological exercises that help children learn speech patterns and motor skills.

- As your baby is developing his language skills, he will enjoy discovering all the many things that he can do with his mouth.

- Pick a song that your little one enjoys hearing. Some popular ones are "Twinkle, Twinkle, Little Star;" "The Itsy, Bitsy Spider;" and "This Old Man."

- Sing the song in different ways. Sing it in a high voice, a whispering voice, a humming voice, etc.

- The more ways your baby hears this song, the more he will try to copy you and develop his language skills.

114

The link between music and spatial reasoning is significant because spatial reasoning skills are part of abstract reasoning.

Itsy Bitsy

■ The song "Itsy Bitsy Spider" is an all-time favorite with very young children.

■ Adapt this song and change the word "spider" to a different and familiar animal that your baby recognizes, such as a dog.

The itsy bitsy doggie

Climbed up the water spout. (walk like a dog and bark)

Down came the rain and washed the doggie out. (fall down to the ground)

Out came the sun (make the sun with your arms in a circle above your head)

And dried up all the rain.

And the itsy bitsy doggie climbed up the spout again. (walk like a dog and bark)

■ Try singing the song using the words pig, cow, and other animal names that your baby knows.

A Twinkle Game

115

WHAT BRAIN RESEARCH SAYS

Research confirms that the highest level of music aptitude occurs immediately after birth. Infants possess an abundance of genes and synapses that immediately make them ready for learning music.

■ Music organizes the rhythm of language.

■ Sit your baby on your lap facing you. This is easiest to do if you are sitting on the floor.

■ Sing the song "Twinkle, Twinkle, Little Star" while you are holding your baby's hands.

■ On the last word of each line, clap his hands together as you emphasize the word a little louder than the others.

> *Twinkle, twinkle, little STAR, (clap hands)*
>
> *How I wonder what you ARE! (clap hands)*
>
> *Up above the earth so HIGH. (clap hands)*
>
> *Like a diamond in the SKY. (clap hands)*
>
> *Twinkle, twinkle, little STAR, (clap hands)*
>
> *How I wonder what you ARE! (clap hands)*

116

WHAT BRAIN RESEARCH SAYS

Talking, reading, and singing to your baby will have lifelong effects on his brain development.

Feelings With Music

- Singing about feelings will help your infant understand the language and expression of feelings.

- Sing the following to the tune of "Frere Jacque":

    Are you happy, are you happy?

    Yes, I am, yes, I am.

    Happy, happy, happy

    Happy, happy, happy

    Smile, smile, smile

    Smile, smile smile. (sing with a happy, smiling face)

    Are you silly, are you silly...continue the verse, singing with a silly face.

    Are you mad, are you mad...continue the verse, singing with a mad face.

    Are you sad, are you sad...continue the verse, singing with a sad face.

- You can also play this game with motor skills such as jumping, running, and marching.

First Sounds

WHAT BRAIN RESEARCH SAYS

A higher pitch captures a child's attention. Speaking more slowly, and with careful enunciation, makes it easier for the baby to distinguish individual words.

- The first sounds that your baby will probably make are *p*, *m*, *b*, and *d*.

- When you respond to those sounds, he will keep making them over and over.

- Copy your little one's sounds and repeat them.

- Sing favorite songs just using the sounds that he makes.

- When you speak to your baby in a high-pitched voice (called parentese), he will listen even more closely.

- Tape record his wonderful babbling sounds. You will be thrilled to have these recordings in later years.

Chin, Cheek, Chair

**WHAT BRAIN
RESEARCH SAYS**

A child who is
talked to often
and sensitively
is more likely to
develop a
capacity for the
complex use of
language.

■ Sing each line of the following poem to the tune of "The Farmer in the Dell":

My chin, my cheek, my chair
My chin, my cheek, my chair
Hi ho the derry o
My chin, my cheek, my chair.

■ Touch your chin, cheek, and the chair when you sing the words.

■ Sing another verse with my head, my heels, my hair.

■ Sing another with my knees, my neck, my nose.

■ This is a wonderful language experience.

Say It Again

WHAT BRAIN RESEARCH SAYS

Talking to babies encourages the development of a good vocabulary in the future.

■ Imitation is a natural skill that babies do very well.

■ Say a word and encourage your baby to copy you.

■ Pick words that he is familiar with and start with one syllable.

■ You've probably already done this by teaching your baby, "What does the cow say?"

■ Each time your baby repeats what you say, praise him and give him a hug.

■ Some easy words are baby, daddy, mommy, apple, light, cat, and bye-bye.

120

WHAT BRAIN RESEARCH SAYS

Love is a powerful connection for a child. The expressions of that love will affect the way his brain makes connections.

The Teeth Rhyme

- This is one of those games that babies love and may use to show off to your friend and relatives.

- Teach your baby to open his mouth and show his teeth.

- Stick out your tongue and see if your baby copies you.

- Now, take your tongue and rub it against your upper teeth.

- Say the following rhyme and do the actions:

    Four and twenty white horses, (point to your teeth)
    Standing in a stall.
    Out came a red bull, (stick out your tongue)
    And licked them all. (lick your upper teeth with your tongue)

- Say it again and point to your baby's teeth and tongue.

- Encourage your baby to stick out his tongue and try to lick his upper teeth.

Jack in the Box

WHAT BRAIN RESEARCH SAYS

Blocks, art, and pretending all help children develop curiosity, language, problem-solving skills, and mathematical skills.

- This popular game helps reinforce the idea that surprises can be fun.

- Make a fist with both hands and tuck your thumb under the fingers.

- On the words "yes I will," pop up your thumbs.

    Jack in the box sits so still.

    Won't you come out?

    Yes, I will.

- Help your child make a fist and show him how to pop up his thumb.

- You can also play this game by crouching down and jumping up.

A Stroller Game

**WHAT BRAIN
RESEARCH SAYS**

Through the wonder of PET scans, scientists have learned that the part of the brain that stores memory becomes fully functional at nine to ten months.

- Take your baby outside and help him sort out the environment. Even though there is much to see, help him focus on one thing at a time.

- Push the stroller along and stop at interesting things to talk about.

- Stop at a tree and talk about the leaves. Let your little one touch the leaves.

- Look for birds or squirrels in the trees.

- Talk about just three or four things on your walk.

- Repeat this game several times, pointing out the same three or four things before you add new ones.

Discovering Books

WHAT BRAIN RESEARCH SAYS

The language journey starts in the womb, where the fetus constantly hears the sounds of his mother's voice.

■ Reading aloud is a wonderful gift that you can give your child.

■ Infants are interested in pictures, the shape of the book, turning the pages, and holding and touching a book.

■ Point to a picture and tell what it is. When you point to the same picture several times, your child will learn the name of the object or person.

■ Ask your child, "Where is the _____?" See if he will point to the picture.

■ Let your baby hold, drop, and turn the pages of a book. This kind of experimentation sets the path for good speech, reading, and special times with you and your child.

■ Read the same book over and over many times.

124

Grocery Shopping

■ Taking your baby to the supermarket can be a pleasant experience if you think of it as an outing for both of you.

■ Here are some things to do with your baby while at the supermarket:

✓ Point out pictures and letters on the cans and boxes.
✓ Show her the foods that she eats and drinks at home.
✓ Go to the produce department and talk about the fruits and vegetables.
✓ Let her put some of the items that you buy into the grocery cart.
✓ Describe foods as you put them in the cart as hot, cold, soft, chewy, crunchy, etc.

Happy Face

WHAT BRAIN RESEARCH SAYS

Researchers have found that children are better at recalling stories that aroused strong feelings in them.

- Given the power of combining stories with feelings, encourage your baby to express feelings.

- Find pictures in magazines of children laughing and smiling. Color pictures are the best.

- Mount these pictures on cardboard and look at them with your baby.

- Talk about the feelings portrayed in the pictures. A happy face will become cemented in your baby's mind and will make new connections in the brain.

- Look at the happy face pictures with your baby and sing a song (any song!) while smiling.

Bibliography

BOOKS

Caine, Geoffrey and Renate Caine. *Making Connections: Teaching and the Human Brain.* Chicago: Addison-Wesley, 1994. Fascinating information to learn more about brain research.

Carnegie Corporation of New York. *Starting Points: Meeting the Needs of Our Youngest Children.* New York: Carnegie Corporation, 1994. A task force of educators throughout the country discusses many areas of developmental growth.

Kotulak, Ronald. *Inside the Brain: Revolutionary Discoveries of How the Mind Works.* Kansas City, MO: Andrews and McMeel, 1996. Reinforces the importance of early experiences and the development of the brain.

Shore, Rima. *Rethinking the Brain: New Insights into Early Development.* New York: Families and Work Institute, 1997. This book explains in lay terms the findings of recent brain research, and what the findings can mean for parents and teachers.

Sylwester, Robert. *A Celebration of Neurons: An Educator's Guide to the Human Brain.* Alexandria, VA: Association for Supervision and Curriculum Development, 1995. Emphasizes how schools produce an atmosphere for learning. Also focuses on positive social contacts and joyful feelings.

VIDEOS

10 Things Every Child Needs The Crucial Role that Parents Play in Children's Brain Development, Chicago: McCormick Tribune Foundation. Shows how the earliest interactions with children can influence brain development and promote social, emotional, and intellectual growth.

Common Miracles: The New American Revolution in Learning. Peter Jennings and Bill Blakemore, ABC News Special, 60 minutes in length. Reveals how we can enable children to uncover their special strengths and become eager learners. A must-see if you care about children and education.

I am Your Child: The First Years Last Forever
http://www.iamyourchild.org. A wonderful video about the new
brain research and how parents and teachers can encourage a
child's healthy development.

Your Child's Brain ABC-20/20. A wonderful overview of what we
know about the brain today. Can be ordered from ABC.

ARTICLES

Adler, Eric. "Baby Talk: Babies Learn Language Early in Surprisingly
Sophisticated Ways." *Kansas City Star* (November 12, 1995).

Begley, Sharon. "Mapping the Brain." *Newsweek* (April, 1992). Shows
how different activities affect the various parts of the brain.

Begley, Sharon. "Your Child's Brain: How Kids are Wired for Music,
Math and Emotions." *Newsweek* (February 19, 1996): 55-58.
Emphasizes the new research on the neural connections that
form in a child's brain.

Begley, Sharon. "How to Build a Baby's Brain." *Newsweek*
(Spring/Summer 1997, Special Edition): 12-32. Describes how
early experiences are essential to stimulate the newborn's brain.

Brownlee, Shannon. "Baby Talk," *U.S.News and World Report* (June
15, 1998): 48-55. Research shows that learning language is an
extraordinary act of brain computation in infants.

Jabs, C. "Your Baby's Brain Power," *Working Mother Magazine* 24-
28. Helps working mothers understand the importance of interactions with young children.

Nash, Madeline. "Fertile Minds," *Time* (February 3, 1997): 48-63. A
fascinating description of how the brain gets wired for vision, language, feelings, and movement for infants.

Schiller, Pam. "Brain Development Research: Support and
Challenges." *Child Care Information Exchange* (September, 1997).

Simmons, Tim and Ruth Sheehan. "Too Little to Late." *The News
and Observer*. Raleigh, NC (February 16, 1997). Reinforces all
that we are currently learning about the brain.

Viadero, Debra. "Brain Trust." *Education Week* (September 18,
1996).

Index